FRAGRANCE OF LIFE

Poetic Reflections

By

C.R. PARAMESH, Ph.D.

Manufactured in the United States of America

ISBN No. 1-58597-005-0

Library of Congress Catalog Card No. 99-96360

Cover photographs by Robert Rein and Balaji Ramarao

Leathers Publishing
4500 College Blvd.
Leawood, KS 66211

About This Book

Here is a book that is unlike others in content and style. Some poems are based on my life experience, some are reflections on life, some are made up, and some distorted, and fabricated for humor, and for introspection on the nature of human mind.

For their help in the preparation of this book
My sincere thanks to my wife Jaya,
daughter Kalpana
and Arun Murali —.

CONTENTS

Hobby Discovered

Day was, I was retiring merrier
After years of a long career.
Friends were kindled by curiosity
If my plan had any grandiosity.

Time to spend was in plenty;
I had no idea how to make it dainty.
Some quipped if I had any hobby
I could not choose one without a lobby.

Day was, I went on a long trip
To see my grandbaby in a crib.
Flying back several hundred miles,
My mind pondered in memory piles.

That was it, I thought I got bit
By none but a hobby that me fit.
Inspired, started writing my feelings;
That gave me unlimited joy and healing.

This journey into an unknown arena
Turned into an intuitive nirvana.
All I did was to open my mind;
Like a parachute it opened unwound.

Who Am I?

Started as a serene, tiny dot,
I grew up in a small spot.
Eyes, nose and all other organs
Became the person, foregone.

Mom had months to contend,
Waited for the nine months to end.
Mom wished for my early arrival
If there was little risk for survival.

I kicked around, moved and crawled,
Had no coach to yell or brawl.
Guessing, I heard some faint noises;
I was not a psychotic, hearing voices.

Been naughty, wondered about welcome,
It was an anxious time for significant some.
It was my time to come out late tonight;
Folks were waiting for a celestial delight.

Agony and pain came to a full halt
When I came out nameless like a bolt.
One and all were ecstatic at the sight;
As I cried, their faces lit like radiant light.

I Could Not Cry

Little baby, I was born
To a loving couple in a rural barn.
Dreams they had were high,
Not knowing Mother would soon die.

I could not cry or feel her absence;
I was too little, knew not her presence.
Alive, she would not have let me cry;
Dead, she could not know I did not cry.

I was not adopted or slighted,
Grandma raised me right.
Grew up enjoying usual fun,
Did nothing to fear or shun.

Played my role with a smile,
Lived up to her hopes in style.
Motherless, but turned out well
To the envy of everyone else.

Am I vain? Who is to judge?
Not I the judged.

I Love Her Face

I love her face serene
That I have not ever seen.
I cannot seem to easily erase;
It dances right before my face.

Trying hard to find a person
Who would fit my impressions,
Distressed, I must learn to focus
On ways to bring her to my locus.

Thought is the medium
Where I pictured her.
Canvas is the medium
Where I captured her.

Now I could find someone
Resembling the painted one.
She would be my Icon right;
I could never let her out of sight.

Strange I should think of it now;
She looks much like the mom I know.

Number Game

What is in a number
That bugs any member?
It may even be a zero.
Miss it, you will regret tomorrow.

What if one plus two is not three,
Does it mean I am not diaper free?
Should two plus three be five,
Am I through with kinder high?

May I count three plus four as seven
And still call it even?
If four plus five is nine,
Do I get to cross the line?

Since five plus six is eleven,
I can only be driven.
Six plus seven is only thirteen;
Wait for driving until sixteen.

Thanks for seven and eight to be fifteen;
High school doors close in on my teen.

If eight plus nine is seventeen,
I am no more in the boisterous scene.

Nine and ten,
Where is the den?
I am ready at nineteen
For a beer at college canteen.

Zero Works in Mysterious Ways

Zero works in mysterious ways,
Touching our lives in subtle ways.
Some believe they are zero
While being in some ways heroes.

Here is a very bright student
Who needs to be prudent.
If he does not get A's every time,
Believes he is a zero all the time.
Others say he is obsessed. Is he?

A smart girl she is with pretty looks;
She knows she is wedded to books,
Craves to be thinner and thinner
Or else believes she is a zero, not leaner.
Others say she is an anorexic. Is she?

He is an intelligent guy in late teens,
Prides meeting want by any means.
If he cannot rob or make a big steal,
Believes he is a zero, no zeal.
Others say he is a criminal. Is he?

She is young, married for years,
All of it severely battered in tears.
Thinks of severing ties and prays,
Believes she is a zero with him stays.
Others say she is of low esteem. Is she?

As a zero I feel needlessly down;
It is your thinking that is not grown.
Take it all in good stride;
Get up and go with real pride.

Calms Your Mind

Poetry lives forever,
Shedding its beauty never.
Does not have to make good sense;
You can indulge in just pretense.
You do not need much to mean,
You still can view all the scenes.

It unfolds the buried mystery,
Makes not much of history.
Never does it cease to amaze
Folks who flock to embrace.

An expression of inner self,
It speaks well for itself.

Start reading as a chore,
Children soon ask for more.
Read for fun and rhyme
Before they do it for dime.

Read as a fan
    If you can.

Calms your mind
    If you can find.

Money Talks

You are all I have got,
I have heard you say that a lot.
Do you love me for what I am
Or is it what I do when in a jam?

Honesty and trust are my traits,
I never fail to be straight.
I keep my promise, am immortal,
But you all are always mortal.

I buy all you want;
Never did I ever say, won't.
Bail you out; I am for hire
When you are in need, dire.
I pay all your taxes with grace
And keep you out of any disgrace.

For all that you treat me as a foe
While I do my best to keep my vow.

For years you lock me up slumped,
But I do give you interest in lumps.

Breathing down neck has been your job,
Holding me in wallet or purse as I sob.
I sob, too, over your conduct mystic
In your delight carrying a silly plastic.

I get to be even looted and stolen,
Unlike you, will never be a felon.
Aye, I am all yours for what you have;
I will become all hers, if you misbehave.

Exit Only

Signs exist in many forms
They are of course within norms.
Signs are in colors, letters, or numbers
Telling us to follow, to remember.

Exit, entrance and other signs, many
Are bright and flashy in colors, any.
Signs are fine, not in vain
It is not hard for one to explain.

"Exit Only" sign I see on the right
At a cemetery shining bright.
"Entrance" sign is missing, obvious
One would not enter unless conspicuous.

Have you ever seen a person dead
Sneak out by "Exit Only" when in bed?
If one should, should one not be told
There is for safety an "EXIT ONLY" bold.

Tryst with Death

Death will find me
        More than I want to see.
No tossing, turning or pill,
The bed will ever remain still.

Voices will no more be heard
Of the dearest by me reared;
Beauty shall no more be seen,
No song or drum heard as had been.

I will feel no pleasure or pain,
Neither know your pain or gain.
I will not know if it rained,
But I know my life was not in vain.

All will miss my familiar face,
Wondering whither I did pace.
No place to go on a long drive
Other than being last driven.

Even the thought of this thought
Makes me choke to a halt.
Do not like tryst with death,
It is no occasion for mirth.
Do I have any say?
None, of course, on this day.

Feelings of some I may have hurt,
Even my dearest wife's in spurt.
Should there be some last say,
Forgiveness is all I pray.

Mom: Where Are You?

FOR VISALAKSHI

Mom, where are you?
I am looking for you.
When I first cried "Ma"
You were there for me.
You looked at me, smiled at me,
You hugged me tenderly.
The warmth of your hug
Was more than physical;
Look on your face
I could not fathom,
But I knew you inspired me.

You talked to me a great deal;
Did you know I would feel?
You did feed me on time,
Did you feel my hunger, too?
That is the mother I know;
Mom, where are you?

I said "Hi-Mommy" overtime,
In your absence you were present;
In my silence I was present,
We did not mean to be reticent.
My feelings beamed on you,
So did yours on me;
It was a divine bonding of us,
How could you hide away?

I am all you wanted,
Am I not you? Are you not me?
My heart aches for you;
I need you more than you know.
That is the mother I know.
Mom, where are you?

Wandering all alone
I looked for you weeping
In the basement, even in the attic.
I missed your loving face
That I kissed many a time.

I could not hear your sweet voice
That sang the lullaby,
Nor could I smell your perfume
That made me feel heavenly.

Tucking me in bed,
Read to me stories and tale,
You were wonderful all the time;
Never knew you tired, growing old,
That is the mother I know.
Mom, where are you?

I know you are proud of me,
I know how much you love me.
Do you not want to see my kids?
You must see my kids' kids, too.

Am I to give up on you?
You taught me more than that.
No, I cannot give up; I will not;
Have I not grieved enough
Looking for you all over?
Can you not heal my pain?
I will cry for you, keep on crying;
You cry for me, prying.
That is the mother I know.
Mom, where are you?

It is not fair
If we cannot share.
Show up, Mom,
I know you love me.
That is the mother I know.
Mom, where are you?

When I am ailing
You cannot away sail;
Soon I will move
Into your attic of love.

I Was Not Strong

I was not strong,
Did some wrong;
I could not see
I was deep in the sea.

I could not contain
Nor maintain,
Told a select few
Who I thought would review.

Hoped they would hold
And none would be told,
But they could not keep mum,
It made me numb.

The world came to hear
And see all my tears.

Mom alone was there to console
My inner soul's soul.

Mirror Error

Mirror, mirror,
You are in error.
I see right shown on left;
I see left shown on right;
You insist that is right,
I cannot help not to fight.

If you are right,
You can keep it right.
If you are not right,
Can you put it right?

I cannot figure it as of yet,
Need time to check it out.
You would still call it that
Until the end of this chat.

I see my body and the beautiful face
With no less than full grace.
I see my eyes, nose or what you may call,
But I am not just the sum of all.

You show every little crease and grain;
There is no trace of my smart brain.

Journalist That I Am

The journalist that I am,
I need know the entire scam.
In the name of people's right
I will make known all straight.
Rumors are checked with tact
Prior to validation as fact.

I do not seed or breed,
I do heed, try to speed.
For a while I may quit
And come up with the best fit.

I am not tumbleweed
Picking up all events to feed.
I do not let known my views
To be a part of the day's news,
Nor do I make up a cast
For a prime time broadcast.
I do not wage a war to tell;
Talking of "Wag the Dog" is swell.

I do not mean to sound altruistic
Nor want to end up a mystic.
Do not laugh or scorn at me,
I only do the job for thee.

Is Present an Illusion?

Can you trust the future
As it is not here yet?

If it is here now,
It is not a future.

The moment it is here
It is a past, not a present.

If what is, is an instant past
And future is past prospective
What then is the present?

Is present an illusion?

He Thinks, She Thinks

You may want to assert;
Better yet be artful to skirt.,
Do not mean wearing one,
Learn to flank for fun.

You are what you think;
Here are a few not to blink.

She thinks I am a leader,
    I say she is the feeder.
She thinks I am the man,
    I say she is the "woo man."

She thinks I am a spender,
    I say she is the lender.
She thinks I love money,
    I say she is my honey.

She thinks I am defensive,
    I say she is pensive.
She thinks I am lonesome,
    I say she is awesome.

She thinks I am a bore,
    I say I you adore.

Doctor's Pills

I am a little girl who is a bit sick,
Better for the doctor to have it fixed.
The doctor is out for a short while,
Would you believe I wait with a smile?

He should be back in pretty soon,
I could see him well before noon.
Here comes the doctor, I like to speak,
Who can cure me by a tender stroke.

I know I am grouchy and ill
'Cause I went out in weather chill.

I soon would feel like a million bucks,
But I cannot leave it all to luck.
First I need to cover myself well
And take the pills as the doctor tells.

Dream On

Day one, a sweet dream born;
Woke up, it was gone in the morn.

A new dream tomorrow,
Hopefully, not about sorrow.

It is only day three,
You dream on all night, free.

Dream on; dream on, it is day four;
Oh! You may instead have a nightmare.

Fifth day of the long week,
You bet, the dream would be bleak.

Dreams seem to come in stream,
But prefer to be lost in daydream.

Children Are Fine

Children are fine
As long as they are mine.
Children do not bother
About the role of the other.

They do not need a dad
Who has abused them bad.
If you should at all doubt,
Do check out the tout.

Why give rights of visitation
To one with no compunction?
Displays superficial charm
To get closer to do harm.
He may present to be nice,
Hidden character is vice.

Should there not be a choice
For the children to voice?

Birds on a Cloudy Day

It was a cloudy day;
The sun was hiding stray,
Peeping off and on, taking rest
Like little sparrows in the nest.

The sky was dark blue,
The ocean was gloomy,
A lonely bird circling around
Like on a merry-go-round.

Yet no bird in sky was seen
In the vicinity she had been.
The loner seemed lost in a race,
Lost directions in outer space.

Or was she seeking a loving mate,
The day being cool for a cozy chat?
Or did she lose her recent mate
Who had been in the trip her date?

Sighting her from a cloud hidden
Flew down her mate in a sudden.
It was a lesson on flying a pair,
They flew chatting romantic affair.

Losing you I felt deeply sad,
Thought of many things bad.
Flying alone I lost being smart,
Feared we were miles apart.

The day was getting darker
Ocean seemed larger.
It was the scariest night
Until at last you came into my sight.

Birthday Greetings

A day older
Than yester;
A year wiser
Than yester.

Dream all you want
Not be daunted;
Set no limits
To reach the summit.

Do it the right way
With no dismay;
Years will run
With exciting fun.

Wish you the best
Forever to last.

Happy Birthday
With Love I Say!

A Darling Daisy

A little girl, Sarita made us all glad,
A joyous season that we then had.
Doubtless, our joy knew no limits,
We saw her soon reach the summit;
She was lovely and cute, a darling daisy,
Who lit our hearts to go crazy.

She could not read then but stories told
Like the one who had a medal of gold;
She would ask us to read and read until
A page skipped she would soon fill.
She was more than a bouncing beauty,
She never was even remotely naughty.

She liked to read and write all day
To delight us before the book she lay;
She learned to sing "Woods are lovely"
With a smile on her face that was lively.

Goats and ducks in parks she liked to feed;
On a day or two, food was not their need.
She felt sad they went hungry;
In her mind this was lingering.
Sarita was the princess to ring the bell,
To win our hearts more than we can tell

Kids in the Pool

Kids in the pool
Do not stay cool.
Shout and jump
Until they slump.

With pride they dive
Under water to hide.
Play hide and seek,
Catch the one meek.

Kids test the peers
For their fear.
Compete for speed,
Racing to be in lead.
Show skills in race
With all the good grace.

Kids do not quit on command
When mom gets to demand.
They try to bend the rules,
But mom could not be fooled.

Marriage Is Sacred

Marriage is absolute,
Love is relative.

Marriage is objective,
Love is subjective.

Marriage is permanent,
Love is transient.

Marriage is sacred,
Love is naked.

Marriage is an investment,
Love is a development.

Marriage is physical science,
Love is liberal arts.

Marriage is a bond-age,
Love is a carriage.

Marriage is a treasure,
Love is a measure.

Marry Now and Love Later

Married a girl afar,
Met her never before.
Folks and I paid a visit,
Neither did union resist.

Our eyes met a few times
All in stealth for a brief time.
Feeling good consent given,
Wedding held tradition driven.
You may at this be shocked;
You cannot however be mocked.

No big qualms heaped
Nor any sobs reaped.
Together for work we went
Day in and day out spent.
Did sightseeing together,
Not holding hands of each other.

Had I ever driven alone,
Would have been a "long goner."
She was the alert navigator,
I was on the accelerator.
Did the driving go smooth?
Not without grinding teeth.

Suppose, I caused some "misery,"
Sure, she did not dislike, says history.
Raised our kids odds to beat
To sit back and watch their feat.

Perfect match? Guess what you may,
Forty-two years should speak a nay.
Sense or nonsense, why not marry now,
Love later, and to stay make a vow.

God, You Have Failed Me

God, You have failed me,
For all I know you would not see.
Angry, saddened and weak,
Fairness is all I seek.

Am I the one doing wrong?
If you can, tell me ere long,
Give me a purpose to adore,
Why am I on Earth a visitor?

Where do I seek thee, tired, sore?
I go knocking every door.
Many kind souls answered my call,
Who they are I cannot recall.
They all have different names,
Look Godly exactly the same.

I say I am in God's hands;
With so many, none for me stands.
I say God willing I be fine,
Never did any hear words of mine.

Have I not spent scores of years
Believing I am God-fearing?
Have I not woven my prayers in song
Hoping you would do no wrong?

Nothing has healed my wound,
Still looking for God to mend.
Hope He/She would not fail
To give me the strength to prevail

And the freedom to sail
With contentment full scale.

Am I the one lonely, in pain?
You are behind every war, insane
You are the divine force
Behind every event's source.

Birth, death, war or poverty count
Are all assigned to your account.

War to control or contain
War for peace to maintain
Is it not insane to do destruction
With lofty aims for construction?

Everything is explained in your name
Do you now see the human play game?

If I am your servant
And you are the savant
How do you see all the events
That go in your account?

None of you in galaxy answered
My prayers, questions uncensored.
Where do I stand in relation to you?
Still waiting to hear if you knew.

What do I claim myself to be?
A divided self with many faces of me.
Is that what You designed?
Or is it gift assigned?

Flattery

Flattery is a delicate skill
You may do well to drill.
It comes not on its own,
There is room to learn.

It has many aliases,
That makes it easy to disguise.
If you are good at this game,
It leaves on you no shame.

Flattering is great,
Flattered is even greater.
Flattery is an intoxicant;
For some it is a repellent.
Too much will boomerang,
Too little will loom around.

Is any one above flattery?
To say "yes" is jittery.
Should the flattered be shrewd,
Flatterer's motive will be nude.

Should you mix it with humility,
You will see combustibility.
It could be a mutual admiration
Based on exaggeration.

It may touch the ego-part;
Do not mistake it for the heart.
Fashionable to say, "I won't kiss."
Life is full of it to not miss.

Teenager Ego

Here I am a smart teenager
Who cannot participate in a wager.
I should be back home I am told
Before it is time for the day to fold.
That is the way my dad has been;
I know he does not really mean.
The court sets curfew as ten,
It is silly to cut me from men.

Do I not have an ego to save
Just as my peers many have?
So I thought and broke the law
Before I knew I was flawed.

It was late when I was picked
To serve time and be licked.
Was it my ego to be displayed
Or was my thinking misplaced?

Should I not get my senses straight,
Regret my wrongs and live right?

Humble Yogi

Up on a majestic hill
Sits a Yogi bachelor, still;
He was handsome and tall,
Renouncing worldly desires, all.

It was a serene, heavenly abode
Wherein his life nothing would erode.
A day dawned, not reckoned as nice,
For his abode had visitors in mice.

Yogi's peace and tranquillity were disturbed,
And he remained seriously perturbed.
His plan to rid the menace of mice
Involved raising a cat that was vice.

Soon he knew the cat liked milk to feed;
He bought a cow to meet this need.
Alas! He realized the cow needed care;
He was worried, puzzled, and scared.

Wisely he hired a woman for this mission
Hoped she would have a clear vision.
Yogi's solitary life grew to a full scale,
Missing only a romantic female.

He pondered and asked in marriage her hand;
Consented, they came tumbling fast to the land.

Timeliness

What is timeliness
If it is not on time?

Is it timeliness
If there is a lapse of time?

What if it is not on time?
It will be untimely.

What if it is not timely?
That will not be in due time.
Is it all the time a question of time?
In course of time it will be overtime.

How come here it is night -time
And elsewhere it is day -time?

It will take up our time,
Let us check the timepiece for the time.

What It Is Not

Selfish is not a fish
You can use in a tank.

Hot dog is not a dog
You can use as a pet.

Hot bed is not a bed
You can sleep on.

Whole is not a hole
Where you can hide.

Pursuit is not a suit
You can wear.

Passage is not a sage
Who can be your guru

Universe is not a verse
You can sing.

Worship is not a ship
That will ever sink.

How Come

If selfish is not a fish,
If hot dog is not a dog,
If hotbed is not a bed,
If whole is not a hole,
If pursuit is not a suit,
If passage is not a sage,
If universe is not a verse,
If worship is not a ship,

How come?
Resemblance is semblance?
Recognition is cognition?

What Ifs

What if man can fly?
Will the bird feel shy?
If a horse can talk,
Will jockey take a walk?

If cow would not like to graze,
Would it not be amazing?
What if bull can be a bear?
Will rodeo bleed tear?

When fish swims fast,
Does turtle feel lost?
If cobra can dance,
Can snake charmer be its fan?

If sea can moan with ups or downs,
Why not my mood go manic or depressed?

Dieter's Delight

Eating is fun for many
But mandated for any.
Diet watchers rejoice skipping
Foods that are scale tipping.

Positive for overweight,
Nothing to lose, you are right;
You may choose to fight,
Better yet, go for food in sight.

Should weight be steady,
Lucky, you need be not greedy.
You may choose to eat all,
You will still be the same girl.

Lean, hungry and feathery,
No harm, indulge in all hickory.

Plenty for dieters to caress,
Herbs and salad sans dressing.

Moonlight Madness

A hot summer day
Special day in May.
Moonlight madness sale
Never gets to be stale.
Not for the sale it makes,
But for the stroll we take.

Sidewalk is not for walk,
It is the place for stops and talk.
Some stroll in colorful shorts,
Checking theirs with others' shorter.
Some are in rolled-up long sleeves
Who were short of short sleeves.

Some attempt at serious display
Of their culinary skills, misplaced.
Time as well for some charity stall
To tap the generous hearts of all.

It is a place to meet in haste
A few city folks not to your taste.

My Kind of Boss

Darling,
You are my kind of boss;
I would love at home to be close.
In work, it is an embarrassment,
Have to sue you for harassment.

I soon would want your post,
Cannot wait for you to be lost.
How could I think so ill
Of one who foots my fat bill?
Can I not wait for a while
And learn to walk in style?

I see him as always grouchy,
He insists I am much too edgy,
He does not like the boss in me;
May be some of me in him I see,
Or am I a little paranoid
Sharing trait of a schizoid?

Snack You Pack

An excellent snack
You need to pack
For a trip to a lake
When you have a break.

Do you know how to make?
I will tell for your sake.

Add flour one cup neat
To one-half cream of wheat.
Mix the two for a union
Adding chopped quarter onion.

Add salt and red pepper to taste
When you want it done in haste.
Mix all with two Tbsp. of oil
And water a little, not spoil.
Work with your hands in a bowl
To make a stiff, workable dough.

In hot oil put dough in small pieces ,
Deep fry to golden brown and recess.

Gossip

Gossip is fun
When loose lips run.
If you cannot spin,
It is no big sin.

Life with rumor will spice up
Like pepper on tender lips.
        If you do not hear one say,
Ask your friend for a hearsay.

Or do an innocent check if true,
Cindy slept with a handsome crew.
Your friend may start to wonder,
Soon she will begin to thunder.

If your day is not full,
You will feel a little dull.
If your day tends to be awful,
No harm in being playful.

Start the rumor tight-lipped,
Whisper to a friend to read your lips.
Now relax and watch the cast,
The day will pass by pretty fast.

Is It True I Can Tell?

Is it true I can tell
Your future that befalls?
If you believe what I tell,
Life will run pretty swell.

What if I cannot share
With the ones I care?
It will be a long mourning
By the end of my journey.

When I tell them "No,"
They do not know I know;
When I do not tell "Yes,"
They think I know less.

What I should say here
Is to so say to be overheard.
That is one way of saying
Without really naying.

Pleased with it as their own,
To others they make it known.
They were not about it kidding,
I was always on it bidding.

Got My Man Back

Still I cannot settle my dispute
With my man of high repute;
We do raise questions to moot,
It gives us something to be hot.

He hedges it is time to pass
That is what he does to harass.
We argue and argue for facts
With no end in sight for a pact.

Love and romance fade away
As we continue in dismay.

Neither knows for sure the basis
For the friction like a crisis.
Once we got to listen to each,
I got my man back with no hitch.

Greed as Weed

I have in me some greed,
It spreads like a garden weed.
It strangles my normal growth,
And I cannot be all I am worth.

Greed grows only when I feed
With thoughts thrown as seed.
What could I do I often wonder,
Not knowing whether to surrender.

No, no, my firm voice tells
And I scratch all my brain cells.
If only I used some good sense,
I could get through the tough fence.
I cleanse my mind of buds, not dwell,
And I do forever feel well.

Visiting a Zoo

A day in September
Was bright and sunny;
I walked to school
With my sister's nanny.
It was no surprise no class was held,
All lined up for a field trip day filled.

It was a long but joyous ride
To see the animals in their hide.
There were plenty to see and fear
Like the lions and snakes, not deer.
I asked the lion if he was the king,
Waited in vain for an answer to ring.

Feeding animals was tabooed and risky;
I did it anyway though it was tricky.
My fingers escaped being bitten,
That put an end to my feeding the kitten.

It was an exciting day with lots of fun,
But the day had to end for us to return.

Was It Hate?

I went to play
With my brother, Ray.
He said no to my friend, Kate
'Cause he said he "hates."

Was it hate
He meant to state?
He could not rate
Or would he debate.

In the end it was not too late
To tell me she refused a date.
We agreed to drop "hate"
And picked up my friend, Kate.

Push Mobile

It was a small, pretty old car,
Not meant to go too far.
Seven of us, all boarded
And the luggage was loaded.

Tried to start by a vigorous choke
Would not budge like it was broke.
Taking turns the kids enjoyed
Pushing it not feeling annoyed.
Elders were ashamed for breakdown
As neighbors watched us headed to town.

It started with a jerk, like it had a fit
Only to raise hopes and instantly quit.
At last the car started to run fast
We all climbed aboard in great haste.

School Days

School is a lot of fun
When there is some bright sun.
Oh, no, today it is raining,
But I have to go happy, feigning.
No, no, it has begun snowing,
But to school I walk groaning.

The cool wind tries to blow me away,
I keep my feet firm from being swayed.
When I reach my school grounds,
There will be kids to play around.

Amanda, my sister, stays home;
She is sick, cannot play any game.
Can I too stay home, play with toys?
Oops! It is not the same as with boys.
Friends at school will miss me a lot;
School days are more fun than not.

Boys Are Boys

Boys were five and seven,
Games were their heaven.
Sun, rain or wind,
Boys were in the yard behind.
Playing all day long
Was not for them wrong.

One favorite was marble,
With break, a meal to gobble.

Marbles in right pocket,
Marbles in left pocket,
Pulling them to slump,
Showing signs of a hump.

Head was like a bun
Toasted by oven, the sun.
Skin was the brown cover
That turned into dark color.

Mommy would at top yell,
Brother would not pause or tell.
Goal was to quietly fill
Their pockets to the full.
Winning was on a hot day
Great for the morn of May.

Have you not had this little fun?
If not, let it in your family run.

Wise Father

One day, a wise father
Asked his two sons to gather,
Told them he was getting ill fast
And may soon breathe his last.

He said he had a large estate
He needed to part in haste.
He gave his sons an apple each
To eat where no one watched.

Puzzled by the task they faced,
Figured, and went to lonely places.
One at last ate the apple and returned,
Came the other with the apple, stunned.

As each told his story,
It was heard with some worry.
One with the apple said in low tone,
Wherever he tried to do it alone,
Someone was always there, like a clone
He the rest of the story etched in stone.

Darling Doubtless

Dear Darling Doubtless,
One word to describe is "Speechless."
With the shining of the moon
The night looked like noon.
Sky was littered with stars twinkling
Like your diamond ring dazzling.

The City of Marrywish
Must be seen by all, is my wish.
It has a Myrtle-like beach
Where one can find a peach.

Flames have lit my dull life,
I have here the time of my life.
Nothing more to tell a distant wife
Except, I wish you were her (e)!

I wish you were her (e)!

Cannot See You Anymore

You know that I know.
I know that you know.
I cannot see you anymore,
But you can see the kids far more
Than wanting to see me some more.

You say you cannot see kids anymore,
They cannot take it anymore.
When they grow up some more,
May be would need you no more.

You say you cannot see me anymore,
But, Honey, I seek you more and more.
I know I too want more than more,
But it is good to wait a little more.

Oh, no! We have wasted lot more,
Time to shut the door all the more;
I mean the door on " Anymore."

Grandma: The Wise Woman

She was a lady, old and wise,
In her seventies and rising.
She meant to me all I needed;
In her care, I grew up seeded
To be what I can best be.

One morning I had a hiccup,
It never ceased to give up;
Grandma's eyes caught my plight.
Raising her voice she yelled at my sight,
"Did you take money from my purse,
I seem to miss a few dollars, yes."
"Oh, Ma, no, never would I steal,"
"I swear I never touched it at all."

No one knew what had happened;
Hiccup for sure was gone dead end.
That was the type of shock treatment
Grandma coughed up for my ailment.

Talking of Age

It strikes me as odd
When poets talk of people old.
Were poets' lives so marred
Or was it they were scared?

Talking of age,
They seem to dread old age.
One wonders at old age,
Seemingly a sad stage.

When I am old
I will still be the same dad
And the same granddad.
I may be bald,
Teeth may be of gold;
You know I will be wiser,
Do not see me as a miser.

No more learning,
Nor need earning.
Do not have to fake
For anyone's sake.

I will have no boss,
That is not a loss.
Am I going to be told
"Fired" because I am old?

I make my agenda
That fits my calendar.
Free for a pleasant walk
With friends as we talk.

I hang my hat on the same rack
For all to know I am back.
In morning coffee meet
Never miss my usual seat.

If old age is scary
How come one gets to marry?

          Death is not to be dreaded, some say
Growing old should be applauded, I say

Travel by Train

The train was about to whistle;
People were still hustling.
The coach was well nigh full,
Many were yet rushing to fill.
Some on board were stiff-collared,
They made up of all sizes and colors.

There showed up a man big and tall
With many pieces of luggage to haul.
He started shoving them in hole
Wherever he could manage to roll.
He then squeezed in a long seat
And went to sleep on the beat.

Then came a man wearing a long beard
With guitar on shoulder looking weird.
Shoved by me, seated half on my lap,
Tuned the guitar, as I collapsed.

Interesting guy was the one, shrewd,
Who never paid heed to any feud.
He went right to his seat with a mission,
Woke up at his station with a "train vision."

Fascinating fellow was the one handsome,
Smart, astute and lonesome.
He never ceased to rattle my tired brain
With his humor and stories of trains,
Their schedules and late arrivals.

No small wonder I was lucky to survive.

What Is in a Dress

What is in a dress
You feel impressed?
Beauty dressed dress
Lets my beauty crushed.

Better buy a dress deaden
So I may look golden.
Price is a factor,
Cannot say does not matter.
Do not like it cheap,
It would be a big leap.

I like designer label
Up front as a rebel.

Dress has to flow
Letting my body glow.
Less it covers body parts,
More expensive, nets more hearts.

Can dress be undone
So Nature and I be one?

Back to My Youth

Do I want to trade
My youth for a man's parade?
        Not man yet to be a man,
Did not live high school years I can.
Missed being a scout or a band player,
        How could my life be saner?

Missed all the fun in the years past,
I asked to go back to my youth at last.
Wondered why I was sick this long;
Now I know my illness cannot prolong.

I waited years within the walls,
Hoping for release to folks in fall.
Give me a few missed years
To wipe off those lost in tears.

I may take time to catch up;
Bear with, not hurry me up.
Longer the youth, the better;
Being a man is tougher.

I wish to snap out to be young
And back to manhood ere long.
I would be fair in paying my due
To rid repression overdue.

Had it not been for this bane,
You would see me graceful and sane.

Discount Divorce

Do not knock on the door anymore;
Get away before I yell some more.
You pose to be a genteel thief;
You sure will end up in great grief.
Do not knock on the door, anymore.

I am not here with a pistol or gun;
I wish you would quietly let me in.
I am not here for your money
Or do I intend to harm you, honey.
All I want is your tender heart
If only you will let it part.

Do not break the door, wait;
Let me get it to you straight.
Do not know if my feelings can open
To an unknown guy if it does happen.
You have a way with words,
Will deed match your words?

Why not you move to the side;
I need to see if you have lied.
Oh, boy! I did not know it was you, boozer;
We have been divorced twice before, loser.

Honey, I can arrange divorce on discount;
You need have no worry on that account.

Do Not Take Away My Child

Do not take away my child,
It will drive me wild.
She is not a toy on layaway;
Before I call the cop, get away.

Yes, I am single, I do her own
For all the reasons known.
What say you the reason
That will convince this person?

Surely for one, I will be lonely ;
She is my pride princess, finally.
Certain that I will be nobody
Unless she remains my sole buddy.

She is all I have got;
I took care of her a lot.
Has she ever known
A baby sitter of her own?

Has there been a morn
When I ever did scorn?
Has there been a say
She missed a school day?

Why do you keep knocking?
Did you come for mocking?
Good heavens, it is a nightmare!
What a relief, not a real scare.

Worry

Tell me your worries,
You will discover who you are.

Worry if you do something,
Worry if you do not.

Worry about what you have,
Worry about what you do not.

Worry about what happened,
Worry about what might happen,
Worry about what did not happen.

Worry is like a rocking chair,
It gives something to do
But it takes you nowhere.

Worry may hurt,
A little worry may be a spurt.

Whether I Tied a Knot

Whether I tied a knot
Or not

I do solemnly swear

In richness and in wealth
Openly or in stealth
          Shall faithfully own
All you saved as your own.

I further solemnly swear

I will fully defend
Without you being offended
Against all vagaries of mind
Of your own or others of a kind.

I do solemnly affirm

Fruits of your labor,
Things you did forever
Will bear your name,
You cannot see as a maim.

He Is Only a Little Boy

Praveen was a little boy
Who is now a great joy.
He is smart and quite bright,
No question he is a delight.
Boys are boys, he seems to ponder,
Letting his folks guess and wonder.

He spoke many words that made sense,
But listener needed to be a little tense.
Of the many words that he gladly spoke,
"Grandpa" was one favorite for his folks.
First sight of a man a little bald,
"Grandpa, Grandpa" was readily called.

He played with his toys, ran the train,
But the one faster was his brain.
Ask him to box his books and toys
He would claim he is only a little boy.
Mommy, Mommy, for help he would cry,
For he knew it was worth a sneaky try.

He loves trucks, mail-vans and cars;
Love for his sister knew no bar.

I Love You, Mommy

In mother's embracing arms
Lies a baby with charm.;
One awaits the other's voice,
Mother to begin was a given choice.

Mom Said:
Sweetie, can we talk?
Ever since your wondrous life began
I have been wanting to hear you say
"I love you, Mommy."
If you did I would say, "I love you, too, sweetie."

Baby Girl said:
I am not going to say anything, Mommy.
You have all you want. I am here with you.

Mom:
Honey, I am proud of you.
What are you saying?

Baby:
I mean what I say, cannot say it aloud.
What do you want, Mommy? Say it aloud.

Mom:
Oh, I want you to say, "I love you,
You are the best mom in the whole world."
I want you to smile, touch my cheeks,
Pull my hair. Keep on looking; I too will be looking
at you all the time. You are my world.

Baby:
Mommy, do you still want all that?

Mom:
Yes, Pumpkin. You are only three months old.
I am going nuts about you. You are my Cinderella.

Baby:
Aren't you already seeing all that in me, Mom?
I did not have to say it. I echo all that in you.

Mom :
I do not know what you are saying, baby.

Baby:
I am just a mirror image of you, Mom.
I am all you are, as loving and beautiful as you are.
Do I have to say it aloud? Did I not convey it to you?

Mom:
I do not know, Princess.

Baby:
Just a minute, Mommy. Something else , too.
You missed it .I am you, part of you, but stand apart, too.
You see, you are able to hug me, kiss me a million times,
Feed me on demand, keep on looking at me tirelessly as I do,
talk to me all the time, sing to me,
'Cause I am in quiet harmony with you.
Can you now see what I am saying?

My silence is speech,
My smile is love,
My eyes are magnetic bonds,
My nothingness is openness.

Thanksgiving: Spare Me!

It is that time of the year
We, turkeys, need to hide in fear.
What do you mean, Dear?
Oh! You do not want to hear.

It is close to Thanksgiving Day,
Better hide or we will be at bay.
How about a protest walk-out?
No, we will all be dead, shot.
May we skip the country
Before we end up as sundry?

We cannot swim, run or fly;
We do not know how to lie.
Could we try to scare their wives
So they may spare our lives?
Let us turn bitter turkeys in haste,
May be they would not bag us to taste.

It is beyond my imagination
Why they target us in this fashion.
We fed them well in desperate times,
Now seduced us, possibly a crime?
They offer grateful thanks
For this ritual, on us they bank.

Let us dare to be true to say
They have been fair until today.
Year round cared for us all the time,
Paid even our insurance on time.

Nursed us in sickness and health;
Only snag is they see us as wealth.
It should make us proud and brave;
You know we do not go to the grave.

Thank them? They let us live until ready
And did not bag us early being greedy.

Sayings Twisted

One swallow is no summer
But it makes a good hummer.

Take the horse to water
But not allow it to trotter.

A stitch in time
Is like gin and lime.

Make hay while the sun shines;
At sun down you may have some to dine.

A bird in the hand, raged,
Is not the same as caged.

Strike while the iron is hot;
Not that it will go rot.

An apple a day
Means, you got to pay.

Prevention is better;
Prohibition is smarter.

Ignorance is bliss,
Not when dating a Miss.

Better be happy than wise,
Both do not go together for guys.

When I Am Dead

When I am dead,
Do I get to see the dead?
Heaven above, will they about me talk?
Before I join, will they to meet me flock?
I know not the truth yet.
When I am dead I am dead, that is set.
To the Dead, matter not it must,
Hell or Heaven, one goes to decay and dust.

If hell (bad) on earth was my life driven,
Up above, anything is a life of heaven.
If heaven (good) on earth was my life liven,
Up above, nothing will suffice unless risen,
For I am dead who needs life be given.

Live in Heaven is far better
Than dead in Heaven, bitter.

If in Heaven, will I get to see
Family and friends talk to me?
Will I get to see them drive on by
Highways and by ways, say bye?

From up above, if I cannot see,
Whither is my being be?
If you know, one amongst you dead,
Please stand up, I say, ere I am dead.

Penny's Pride

I am pretty, small and go around,
        Not that I play a big role around.
Fall is a season of pretty colors;
No contest, I too have shades of color.
        I am a well-known country trotter;
In piggy bank I become a squatter.

You cannot dismiss me without cost,
Do you think I can easily be lost?
You need me to break a tie,
To round it off to dollar without a lie.

You know I make hundred to a dollar;
Alas, others cannot come near my parlor.
Be it known, he who resides in my residence
Is no less than Abraham Lincoln the President.

I do not mean this in jest;
        You know I carry "Liberty"
        And "In God We trust."
You should now know my name,
Can you see my hidden fame?

        May be I am on a little pretense;
I leave it to your good sense.

Nose on My Face

The nose on my face
Is a little bit long;
It is wide at the base,
It fits on my face wrong.

Can I the one barter
With you for the shorter?
That would mean lot better
For us both who are bitter.

Ready for Any

She is filthy rich;
She has a hitch
        Not knowing which
To choose to ditch.

She had no money;
She was not a phony.
It was weird and funny,
She was then ready for any
Who said, "honey."

I Was a Democrat

I was a Democrat
Who was not a hypocrite.
I became a Republican
To be an applicant one
For a position vacant
With the exit of Mr. DoCant.

I am no Mr. DoLittle;
I can try to be a Mr. FairGrant,
Like to have right done;
I do know right is no fun.

I am called an aristocrat,
Rather be one than a bankrupt.

For all you know, labored like an ass;
When I die, glad to escape all I passed.

Is It Fair for the Cows?

People are fond of pets;
Pets help loneliness offset.
It gives a sense of ownership,
Have with them a partnership.
Laws are there to protect
Every form of neglect.

Is it fair for cows in farm
To be left on their own in storm?
Hundreds flock under a tree
As if to talk of being free.

If you could hear them yell,
You know what they would tell.
They are not crying to be fed,
But talk of winter need for a shed.

Do bulls, cows need fight
For a safe Bill of their rights?
Had they had a voice to state,
There would never be any debate.

Cows may not be sacred;
Many are needlessly dead.
Why not fairness prevail
And a new Bill soon unveiled?

My heart bleeds when I see
Voiceless animals in winter debris,
Standing quiet, heads down on peat
Like a prayer group at a meet.

Their prayers seem to deepen
For the Heavens' Gate to open.

A Pair of Shoes

Mommy, your shoes are pretty,
But they are in the closet, I pity.
May I make them feel great
By wearing them bare feet?
No, Dear, your feet are too small;
You may stumble and have a fall.

Mommy, my feet are not small;
The shoes are big and tall.
May I tell them they are cute?
And they do not have to be mute.

Do you shoes feel a bit lonely?
If you shrink, we could ride a pony.

I may be a pair of shoes in your view;
I feel swept off my feet with your news.

Listen to my story:

> I am as cute as you are,
> I come in all pretty colors,
> I even meet every price dollar,
> I walk everyone,
> I go to every party and dance.

That is not all:

If you are home, I am home;
If you run, I run;
If you shine, I shine;
If you walk, I walk.

I will walk with you every stage;
We will be friends through all ages.

Art of Heart

It was like another day;
I went to bed for the day.
It came all of a sudden
That was hitherto hidden.

It came with little warning,
Was enough for mourning.
Shooting pain squeezing the chest;
Strange, it was on the right, not left.
Profuse sweating, not kidding,
Kind of unique pain, not ridding.

Oh, God! It is the heart
That is not working great.
Rushed to the hospital to sort,
Wishing to keep working in part.
Doctors did the checking
As my heart was kicking.

Surgery was imminent;
Mind started reminiscing.
Slowly wheeled into the theatre,
Giving time with the Creator.
Hard to describe the feelings,
Unsure of coming out, wheeling.

Lucky for a by-pass, double,
It was more than I could dribble.
Came out beaming with a smile
For a life of a million miles.

Anorexic's Reflection

I am a girl of sweet sixteen
Weighing a hundred less thirteen.
I felt fine, had no reason to frown
Until one day my friend put me down.

That is not all that I had to face;
My friend thought I was a disgrace.
I could not dance feeling fat,
Made a calorie count whenever I ate.

Every time I counted, less I took
For fear I would lose my perfect look.
Losing a pound a day was a compulsive role;
Reaching "ideal" weight was my defined goal.

Walking down a crimson hallway
I lost one morn my balance halfway,
Could not figure out my way of thinking
Until the therapist started events linking.

It was not like I was overweight,
But I lost sight of what was right.

I Have a Dear Friend

I have a dear friend
Who has a loving wife, kind;
Life's dream is all met
Happy as a lark they wait,
Wait for the soul to rest,
Not push for higher test.

It is funny but true,
They settled on a course sure;
He agreed, she agreed, no lie,
By God's grace she first die.

Is it not strange they have a pact
When no one knows His act?
Show them mercy when alive,
He is no villain with God to vie.

Does he want the House in order
To join in splendor her cadre?
Wake up, my dear friend,
I do not know your mind;
One thing I know, not know what to say
Except that you may be first as always.

I Am Glad I Have Memory Loss

My folks say I am forgetful
And call my condition woeful.
Bewildered by the news, it is serious;
It did not shake me up to be furious.
It is easy for people to call me crazy,
I am not an Alzheimer, only spacey.

I recall I served my country well,
Not a disabled Vet sitting in a cell.
I am accused I throw priced things;
On their own they cannot go, no wings.

My memory displays no big folly
Other than being a usual sloppy.
Is it not sad that I cannot get mad
Or sad at what they say that is bad?
Attention I cannot seem to pay,
Not that I have much to say.

People call me by some sort of a name;
If I remember, that is now not the same.
May be I was all that in recent past,
Do not know what else continues to last.

I am gentle, human and frail,
Unable to follow a simple trail.
How come I can hear or see
But not know, grasp or feel?

How come I wander with no escort,
Do not use even a simple golf cart?

Should it be true, am I a bad person?
Bad, I would rather be a dead person.
As my age advances, dementia haunts;
Living for me gets to be daunting.

People are funny,
Act schizophrenic.
If things are old, they are called antique;
If people are old, they are called geriatric.
If you are a thing, old is gold,
If you are a person, old is "sold."

Oh, God! It is frightening;
I am glad, I have m–e–m–o–r–y loss.

Bed Time

It is time for bed;
The hour is nine.
Tucked in, I said
You will feel fine.
Can I stay a little longer busy?
I am only watching "I love Lucy."

My Brother

I like playing ball
With my brother, Paul.
He would play all day long
But not let me join his gang.

I would fake to start to cry
Until he would say, let us try.
Played and played until mom's call;
That is my brother I turn to, Paul.

He Is the One I Love

He is the one I love,
But I cannot have him now.
He is soon to be married
To a girl who lied.
She managed to catch,
At that I am no match.

I love him for who he is,
Nothing in him I miss.
Why does he not love me?
Or is it that it is not to be?
Why should it be me to cow
And give up my first love?

She loves him for what he is;
Get my drift, do not miss.
Remotely I am aware
Of my feelings of despair;
I feel I am already his,
But he is not mine to kiss.

I may have to lose him
No matter how I see him.
I remain loyal to love;
I hope he may to me bow.

Am I to give him up not
Or am I still crazy to be hot?

Agri-Ugly Culture

Is it agriculture
When you grow marijuana?

Is it agriculture
When you grow poison Ivy?

Do not know what to call it.

If it is not agriculture,
Why not call it ugly culture?

No fun intended,
For I too am your descendent.

Far from the Madding Crowd

It is a pretty little town
Standing in the middle as a crown.
Prairie, pasture and meadow lands
Stretching to the horizon's end.

Plenty of pheasant, quail and rabbit
To meet your long-held sporting habit.
It does not boast of highways or mall;
Pride rests in people and their City Hall.

The city is far from the madding crowd;
It has values hidden to be proud,
Has its share of the veteran honors
With the bombers carrying the banners.

Known for a fort, a National Historic Site
Where you learn of early settlers' fight;
If you are looking to Larned for a trail,
Seek nowhere; follow the Santa Fe Trail.

Nothing you enjoy will be missed in life,
Including the four seasons, tennis and golf.
Nothing you enjoy will be missed in life
Other than the big city stress and strife.

The tranquillity lies in the people's sense
That they are good neighbors with no fence.
Dream on for your kids to be wholesome;
The city will nurture their mind to blossom.

Jewel on a Crown

We flew a thousand mile
Just to see Shannon smile.
Yes, she did smile some;
That was more than wholesome.

She sure has the best smile
That is unique to her style.
Her face lit up with a little frown
Looking like a jewel on a crown.

The sound of her drizzly voice
Was resonant with saint-like poise.
Bright eyes and beauty dressed face
Will ever remain in our memory base.

Blessed are her loving parents,
Not to speak of four grandparents
Waiting for her call by name
Before she goes a mile for fame.

Something Special About Mom's Bed

I began my life as a tiny dot,
Been in mother's womb a lot.
Grew up bigger in the sac
Until in Mom's arms I was back.

In hugging posture she held me tight;
It was tender and warm all night.
Moved from bassinet to a bed, crib,
Looking forward to using a bib.

Crib bared my moves to a few,
Got a bed of my own ere it was due.
It did not seem to fill all my heart,
I longed for Mom's bed being smart.

Often I jumped and rolled fearless
In a safe bed where I felt peerless.
Whether for fun, gossip or sickness,
Mom's bed had all the richness.

The charm was not for a spoiled brat;
The bed for us all was a place to chat.
I cherish the bed as a magic pond
Where my life started goodly grand.

Self Love

I am not the doubter,
I am the doubted.
I say I am just "Me";
Friends say I am more than "Me,"
Do not know why they so judge
And call me self-centered.

Of course, I do love myself ;
Who else will, if I do not?
I am not too grandiose
Or am I self-promoting?
I am driven to pursue,
Do not like to be rescued.

My ego is not inflated;
It is just where it ought to be.

You called me narcissistic;
Darn it, I hope you were not sarcastic!

Truth Family Ties

Truth is pure and simple,
Just as a beautiful temple.
Inside the venerable mansion
Lies a mountain of notion.

In truth, a big family resides
With parents getting to preside.
Siblings and cousins are many
As are members of family, any.

Candor and frankness are doers
Who are the dad and mom in order.
Sincerity and honesty are sisters;
Fact and reality are brothers.

Veracity is only a half-brother
While memory is a big half-sister.
Where are my woodshed cousins?
Afloat all over in country prisons.

Mislead is my missing cousin, Deceive;
Misinform is my cousin's cousin, Confuse;
Omission is my distant cousin, Passover;
Fake is my look-alike cousin, Fudge,
Forsaken not are others or Hedge.

Oh! Forgot, Lie is my new Mistress
I fail always to distrust.

Zero or Hero

If I am a zero,
Will you call me a hero?
If you call me a cipher,
I would think you are a miser.
Do not call me a goose egg
When I am not there to beg.

I may be a zero, just a number,
Not a naught slumberer.
I am active, have my honor
To not fake in any manner.
That tells I am something;
Alas, my maiden name is nothing!

I am elegant and versatile
If you can tap my fertile style.
I cannot take a minus or plus;
I am unique in this class.

Place me to the left of one,
I still stay virgin and none.
Place me to the right of one,
I become a solid ten.
How about between two ones,
You know I am hundred one.

Zero to right, left or middle
Makes a difference in riddle.
You may be a millionaire
Add more zeros, be a billionaire.

Is that all you can borrow
To describe me a powerful zero?
Can you not see me a zero and above
And as in tennis, call me LOVE.

Honey, Hurry Up

"Honey, hurry up, let us not be late,"
Tired of hearing this not to my taste.
Do not know if it reflects my fate,
Never did anytime he say he hates.

Getting ready is not for me easy;
I do need time, as I am fussy.
Apparels in closet for long I stare,
Do not know yet what I should wear.

Hard to decide if blue or gray fits,
Nor can I list the ones that misfit.
You bet at last I settled on a dress;
He did not seem much impressed.

Looked for a matching shoe misplaced,
Shocked it dislodged from its place.
Finally picked my shoes whining,
Not ready for wear without shining.

Closet needs to be meticulous
Or else I feel silly and ridiculous.
I like tidying, showering often a day,
Look for things misplaced every day.

Repeatedly I check the door lock,
Call me compulsive and mock.
No one asked me to be sloppy
I would have even faked and been happy.

No More Deaths or Births

Only a year old, he was fine,
Full of energy, beauty and brain.
All he wanted was to live to full
And make his mission fruitful.

Do wishes run a normal course?
May be so, depending on hidden force.
Alas! For him it was not meant to be.

Like a twinkling star he did die.

Devout parents did all the best,
Left to endure his eternal rest.
His demise met no rule of law
For the innocent with no flaw.

Parents agonized, feeling awful,
Standing at a crossroad mournful.
Is he from above watching them?
Can he possibly forgive them?

Who speaketh the last
For folks like them aghast?
It is not fair for children to die;
Was birth meant to be a lie?

If fantasy were to rule to vie,
God can freeze us all alive.
That would be a static mirth
With no more deaths or births!